Introduction

Two-hundred years ago, a small Welsh [~book~] was published in Carmarthen. Despite its brief and biblically-balanced summary of the Christian Gospel, it created a nationwide furore. Its author was John Roberts, pastor of the Independent Church at Llanbrynmair. A son of Evan and Mary Roberts of Bronyllan, Mochdre, Montgomeryshire, John was born on 25 February 1767. He was one of twelve children.

In his youth, John's parents moved to Llanbrynmair, and joined the old-established Independent church there. John commenced preaching at 'Yr Hen Gapel' in January 1790. In the following March he entered the Oswestry academy. There he came under the influence of Dr Edward Williams (1750–1813). In August 1796, John was ordained as co-pastor of the Llanbrynmair church with the then-aged Richard Tibbot, upon whose death, in March 1798, he became sole pastor. In January 1797 Roberts married Mary Brees of Coed Perfydau, Llanbrynmair. In due time, they were blest with three sons.

In addition to his pastoral work, Roberts kept a day-school at his chapel, and through his diligent efforts six schoolhouses for occasional services and Sunday schools were built within a radius of five miles of Llanbrynmair. In 1806 he settled with his family at a small farm belonging to Sir W. Williams-Wynn of Wynnstay, called Diosg, on the improvement of which he spent much money and energy, though only a tenant from year to year. Harsh treatment was subsequently dealt to him by his landlord and, after his death, to his widow and children, by a rent increase on his own improvements, under threat of a notice to quit. This injustice was made public by his son, Samuel Roberts (1800–1885), in *Diosg Farm: a Sketch of its History* (Newtown, 1854).[1] He died on 21 July 1834, and his monument may be seen in the burial-ground of Yr Hen Gapel.

Roberts was noted for his gentle manner and eminent piety. Influenced in his theological views by Dr Edward Williams, he questioned the exaggerated 'high Calvinist' orthodoxy of the time. Rejecting the tightly-defined doctrine of 'limited atonement', and known consequently as a 'moderate Calvinist', John Roberts expounded his views in *Dybenion Marwolaeth Crist—The Ends of Christ's Death* (Carmarthen, 1814). In the resulting storm of controversy, the author was bitterly assailed by Arminians on the one hand and by ultra-Calvinists on the other. In reply to a critical response from Thomas Jones of Denbigh (who was actually nothing like the more extreme preachers John Elias and Christmas Evans), John Roberts published *Galwad Ddifrifol ar Ymofynwyr am y Gwirionedd*, Dolgelly—*A Serious Call to Inquirers for the Truth* (1820). This work was endorsed by leading Independent ministers, including the great preacher William Williams, Wern.[2]

One of many evidences of the theological ferment of the period was the publication of a translation of four sermons on particular redemption by the English 'High Calvinist' John Hurrion (1675?-1731). Translated into Welsh by Evan Evans of Trefriw, the book carried an arrogant and intemperate introduction by John Elias. The work was intended as a counter-blast to what many felt was an attack on Calvinism by both Arminians *and* the preachers who were embracing the so-called 'New System' teaching of Dr Edward Williams being propagated by John Roberts.[3]

Dr Owen Thomas assessed John Elias's vehement introduction as follows:

> John Elias, as was his custom, made use of strong language in almost infallible tones while presenting his own views of the subject and condemning those who disagreed with him. Very rarely have we come across such unfraternal remarks as those found here, and in such a short piece. We are not surprised that with this introduction he succeeded in hurting the feelings of good men of differing views far more than in confirming others in his own view, let alone winning them over.[4]

Regarding John Roberts's 1814 publication, Dr Owen Thomas expressed surprise that this book of only 24 pages aroused so much virulent opposition. In his opinion, 'there is nothing extreme in the teaching or tone of the book'.[5] The only way he could explain the intense hostility it received was to

conclude 'that the land was to a significant degree leavened with very High Calvinistic ideas'.[6]
English readers may judge the theological merits of John Roberts's work for themselves since *The Ends of Christ's Death*—which first appeared in English in *The Congregational Magazine* in 1825[7]—is now republished.
A decade or so after these heated debates, the seraphic preacher John Jones, Talsarn did for the Calvinistic Methodists what John Roberts, Llanbrynmair and William Williams, Wern had done for the Independents.[8] These servants of Christ liberated Christian people from the tyranny of man-made theological systems! Their views were actually consistent with the teaching of John Calvin, Richard Baxter, Matthew Henry, Isaac Watts, Philip Doddridge, Jonathan Edwards, Daniel Rowland, John Newton and many others. Dr Owen Thomas's monumental survey covers the entire period of these doctrinal disputes within all the denominations of Wales. For a more detailed account of the issues, I refer the reader to my recent biography on John Jones, Talsarn.[9]

Dr Alan C. Clifford

NOTES

[1] See *Dictionary of National Biography* (Oxford: Oxford University Press, 1885-1900), Volume 48.
[2] See Rees, T., *History of Protestant Nonconformity in Wales* (London: John Snow, 1861), 465.
[3] See Owen, W. T., *Edward Williams, DD (1750-1813), His Life, Thought and Influence* (Cardiff: University of Wales Press, 1963), 128.
[4] Thomas, O., tr. John Aaron, *The Atonement Controversy in Welsh Theological Literature and debate, 1707-1841* (Edinburgh: The Banner of Truth Trust, 2002), 88.
[5] Ibid., 161.
[6] Ibid.
[7] 'A Letter to a Friend, on the Designs of the death of Christ', *The Congregational Magazine*, No. 1 (NS), Vol. 8 (December, 1825), 625-30.
[8] See Jones, O., *Some of the Great Preachers of Wales* (London: Passmore & Alabaster, 1885), 315.
[9] See Alan C. Clifford, *John Jones, Talsarn: Pregethwr Y Bobl/The People's Preacher* (Norwich: Charenton Reformed Publishing, 2013).

John Roberts's memorial
Llanbrynmair

ON THE DESIGNS OF THE DEATH OF CHRIST

John Roberts, Llanbrynmair

MY DEAR FRIEND, — When we had the happiness the other evening, of spending a little time together, I understood you were not quite satisfied with what was said respecting the designs of the death of Christ. Therefore the queries proposed in your last afford me much pleasure, as in answering them I shall have an opportunity of expressing my views more fully, though briefly, on this very important subject.

You ask, "Did Christ die for any besides the elect, or, are there any designs to be answered by the death of Christ besides the salvation of the elect?"

It appears to me, that the death of Christ is represented to us in Scripture, as the medium through which all blessings, of every kind, are conferred upon guilty sinners, — that no blessing of any kind is, or can be, enjoyed by men, but in consideration of the mediation of Christ. It was with a particular respect to the sacrifice of Christ, that God has promised us temporal good things. We read of Noah as soon as he was come forth out of the ark, that, by divine direction he built an altar unto the Lord, and took of every clean beast, and of every clean fowl, and offered burnt offerings on the altar. "And the Lord smelled a sweet savour, and the Lord said in his heart, I will not again curse the ground for man's sake,... neither will I again smite any more every living thing as I have done. While the earth remains, seed-time and harvest, and cold and heat, and summer and winter, and day and night, shall not cease" *(Gen. 8: 20-22)*. God could have smelled a sweet savour in these sacrifices, only as they were types of him, who gave himself an offering and sacrifice to God for a sweet smelling savour. Have you not, my friend, been often surprised at the forbearance of God with sinful men? How he has continued to give them fruitful seasons, filling their hearts with food and gladness [*Acts 14: 17*], notwithstanding their great unthankfulness and rebellion? In this, God does not so much regard the unthankfulness and rebellion of those who receive his favours, as he regards his covenant ratified in the death of his dear Son. "And the bow shall be in the cloud, and I will look upon it, that I may remember the everlasting covenant between God and every living creature of all flesh, that is upon the earth" *(Gen. 9: 16)*. O how this consideration should enhance the value of even temporal mercies? They flow unto us through the blood of the cross. And, O, how we depreciate the precious blood of Immanuel, when we abuse them on our lusts, instead of using them to the glory of God!

It is also through the blood, or in consideration of the sacrifice of Christ, that offers of salvation are made unto all who hear the Gospel. I am not acquainted with any belonging to any denomination of Christians, who deny that the calls, invitations, and overtures of the Gospel are addressed to sinners in general. And, indeed, I do not know how it is possible for any professing faith in the Bible to deny this. How could the calls of the Gospel be more general than they are? "Look unto me, and be saved all the ends of the earth." — "Ho, every one that thirsteth, come ye to the waters." — "Compel them to come in." — "Whosoever will, let him come and take of the water of life freely." The Gospel proclaims blessings of infinite value unto every soul, which every way suit his state and condition. The ground and foundation of these gracious calls, invitations, and expostulations, can be no other than the sacrifice of Christ. It is in *his name* we are to preach repentance and forgiveness of sins to all nations. God is *in Christ* reconciling the world to himself, and we are to beseech sinners *in Christ's stead*, to be reconciled on this ground;" for he hath made him to be sin for us who knew no sin." We are to preach the Gospel to every creature; — and to preach the Gospel, is to preach Christ crucified. The sacrifice of Christ is the *foundation*; preaching repentance and forgiveness of sins is the *superstructure*; and how can the superstructure be of greater extent than the foundation? Must not both be commensurate? I am not able to see how the one can be more general than the other. And you know there are the same general expressions used respecting the designs of the death of Christ, as there are to express invitations of the Gospel. "Who gave himself a ransom for *all*." "That he by the grace of God should taste death for *every man*." He is the propitiation "for the sins of the whole world."

But, perhaps you might say, "Though Christ died for none but the elect, yet as we do not know who the elect are, it is right to preach the Gospel to all in his name." If so, *ignorance* is the only ground we have to preach the Gospel to every creature, and a sinner ready to perish has no better ground than *ignorance* to apply unto God, through Christ, for salvation. And is it so, my friend? Have we no better foundation than *ignorance* to preach the Gospel to every creature? To go to the highways and hedges to compel them to come in? Yes, indeed, *we* have. We *know* that the blood of Immanuel has infinite merit — that it is sufficient for all the world. We *know* that *as* Moses lifted up the serpent in the wilderness, even so must the Son of man be lifted up, that whosoever believeth on him should not perish, but have eternal life. We *know* that God sent not his Son into the world to condemn the world, but that the world through him might be saved; and we know that every sinner convinced of his need of salvation, has a foundation firm as the testimony of the Three in heaven, and three on earth, that there is *for him* eternal life in the Son. No one willing to come to God by him can doubt this without a false and injurious reflection on the veracity of the divine word.

If sinners, in general, where the Gospel is preached, do not stand related to the blood of Christ, to use the language of our *Saviour,* if the blood of Christ is not the *great thing that belongs to the salvation of all who hear the Gospel;* Luke 19: 41-2, I do not see how any could be guilty of rejecting it. Rejecting or refusing, supposes that the thing rejected, or refused had been offered to us. Neither do I see *how* any man can be punishable for refusing that which is the property of another. Yet how unspeakably awful are the threatenings denounced against those who reject the Gospel. O! of what vast consequence will the blood of Christ be to us all! What tongue can express, or what heart can endure the unutterable weight of the wrath denounced in that well known passage — "Of how much sorer punishment suppose ye, shall he be thought worthy, who hath trodden under foot the Son of God, and hath counted the blood of the covenant, wherewith he was sanctified, an unholy thing, and hath done despite to the Spirit of Grace!" How deeply are we concerned, lest any of us be profane rejectors of the Gospel, like Esau, who despised and sold his birthright! We have as good a claim to all the blessings freely offered us in the Gospel, as Esau had to the privileges of the first-born, Heb. 12: 16-17. "For, if we sin wilfully after that we have come to the knowledge of the truth, which we all do in the Gospel, except we willingly shut our eyes against the light, there remains no more sacrifice for sin; implying that this sacrifice is sufficient, and within the reach of us all; but a certain fearful looking for of judgement and fiery indignation, which shall devour the adversaries" *(Heb. 10: 26-7).* 1 beg leave to ask, my friend, — Are we to invite all our hearers? Are we to urge them to seek peace with God through Christ? Are we to assure every sinner, or, indeed, can we assure any *sinner,* that God is willing to receive him as such? How can God be willing to receive a sinner without some provision for the honour of his law, and the rights of his government?

You ask again, — "Did not Jesus Christ die for some sinners more particularly than for others?" We are most clearly taught, that as many as shall be finally saved, shall be saved according to the election of grace; and for my own part, I do not know how it is possible for any one sinner to be saved, but according to the purpose of him who worketh all things according to the counsel of his own will. If it be God's work, actually to save *in* time every individual that shall be saved, he must from eternity have *designed* to save every individual that shall be saved. The Scriptures further teach us that there is an especial relation between the whole of the mediation of Christ and the elect. They were chosen *in him.* They were given *unto him.* For their sakes he sanctified himself. They are his seed. His church is his bride, and he gave himself for it. Ephes. 5: 25.

We cannot doubt our blessed Lord, in all his sufferings, viewed *the* elect as a particular part of the reward of his death. He shall possess a seed numerous as the morning dew. He shall see of the *travail* of his soul and be satisfied. But we are not taught to divide the price of redemption, as if we were to say, if I might be allowed the use of such terms to express the gross idea, that he laid down some very great portion of the price for the elect, and some smaller portion for others. No, my friend. The sacrifice of him, who through the eternal Spirit offered himself without spot unto God, is infinite in every respect; and what is infinite cannot be divided. The sacrifice of Christ is the one indivisible consideration, in respect whereof God confers upon men, who have forfeited their right to every favour, all the blessings of every kind they enjoy. According to the good pleasure of his own will, be bestows upon some more valuable blessings than upon others. He bestows temporal good things in various degrees, and, perhaps, some moral means of instruction, upon all in every nation. To *some* nations, he sends the Gospel of the kingdom, which is glad tidings of great joy to every sinner, and unto *some* — even those who have from the beginning been chosen to salvation — he giveth his Holy Spirit to dispose them effectually to believe unto salvation. These are all sovereign favours conferred upon men through the mediation of Jesus Christ.

You further ask, — "If Christ gave himself a ransom for all, or if all who hear the Gospel, stand related to the death of Christ, did not he die in vain with respect to those who do not believe?" God forbid we should suppose that Christ, in any respect, died in vain. The blood of Christ, as well as the Gospel of Christ, will prove a sweet savour unto God to in them that are saved, and in them that perish. None of the works of God will prove vain or abortive with regard to his own glory. He will have a tribute of praise from all his works; but above all, from the stupendous work of Christ's death. The blessed Redeemer's work shall be rewarded with regard to the disobedient. "And now, saith the Lord, that formed me from the womb to be his servant, to bring Jacob again to him; though Israel be not gathered, yet shall I be glorious in the sight of the Lord, and my God shall be my strength." It is a great honour to Christ that his blood is accounted of such value, that in consideration thereof, repentance and forgiveness of sins are proclaimed unto all nations. And though sinners despise the glad tidings, and reject the gracious overtures of the Gospel, yet the Saviour shall be glorified in the righteous punishment that shall fall upon them who neglect so great salvation. All the dealings of God with men, both as a gracious sovereign and a righteous governor, through the mediation of Jesus Christ, will appear unspeakably glorious. Christ shall see of the travail of his soul, not only in the salvation of the elect, but in the display of God's justice in dealing with the wicked.

We are not able to ascertain the extent of the government of Jehovah. Perhaps mankind constitute but a small part of his vast empire. But however extensive his dominion, and however numerous his subjects, may we not gather from Scripture, that all are governed some way through the mediation of Christ? The effects of his death seem to extend to the heavens, as well as to the earth. To what exalted strains doth Paul describe the effects of his death? Col. 1: 20. "And having made peace by the blood of his cross, by him to reconcile all things to himself, by him, I say, whether things on earth, or things in heaven."

You ask — "How is the offer of salvation through the blood of Christ, a blessing to those who reject it, since it is certain their misery will be greater at last, than if such an offer had never been made them?"

You might ask, my friend, with the same propriety, how a strong constitution, good understanding, kind friends, extensive possessions, &c are blessings to those who abuse them? None deny that *these* are valuable blessings, and yet it is certain that the misery of those who abuse them will be greater than if they had not possessed them. We are not to estimate the value of a gift by the manner it may be used or abused by him that receives it. Were you, my friend, to give me a guinea, and were I to spend it for that which would be of no profit to me; would my so spending it lessen the value of your gift? None deny that the Gospel is a great blessing conferred upon men; yet this blessing is abused by thousands, and the misery of such as abuse the Gospel, will certainly be more awful at last than the misery of those who never heard of the Bible. God, as the King of Israel, had a gracious design in giving them right judgements and true laws, good statutes and commandments, that Israel might be a holy and happy people; and those right judgements, true laws, and good statutes, as *objective means*, were infinitely suitable to answer this gracious purpose. Israel would have been a holy and happy people under the good and righteous government of Jehovah, but for their own fault. In all their sufferings they had no one to blame but themselves. It was always their *own wickedness* that corrected them, and their *own backslidings* reproved them. In the same manner, God's design in publishing salvation through Christ to every soul of man is, that all should believe and be saved. God is not willing that any one should disobey the Gospel, and render himself thereby obnoxious to everlasting punishment. God is infinitely good; "he will have all men to be saved and come to the knowledge of the truth." "He is long-suffering to us-ward, not willing that any should perish, but that all should come to repentance." — "As I live saith the Lord, I have no pleasure in the death of the wicked, but that the wicked should turn from his way and live." It is essential to God as a good and righteous governor, to *will* that all subjects of his government should be obedient and happy; he can no more cease to will this, than he can cease to be a good and righteous Governor; and there is all possible objective suitableness in the Gospel to render all that are blessed therewith obedient and happy. There is no let or hindrance visible or invisible, positive or negative, in the way to be so, but their own wickedness.

Perhaps you might be disposed to ask, has God any *will* that goes further than this will, which is essential to him making some of the subjects of his government holy and happy? Yes, certainly, his *sovereign will!* It is essential to every good and righteous governor to *will* the happiness of all his subjects, and to provide them with suitable laws for this purpose; but he might *will* to bestow *royal favours* on *some* of his subjects. The Supreme Governor likewise necessarily *willeth* the happiness of *all* his subjects, and he hath provided them with suitable promises and commandments in the Gospel, as objective means to render them so; but according to his sovereign will he bestows royal favours upon some of the subjects of his government, even upon those he has predestinated to be conformed to the image of his Son.

It appears to me, that in the death of Christ, the most astonishing event that ever took place, God had two designs of distinct consideration, though not inconsistent with each other; the one as *Moral Governor*, which respects the subjects of his government in general, and the other as a *Gracious Sovereign*, which respects the elect in particular; and, indeed, it appears to me that God has these two distinct designs in view, in all his great and public transactions with mankind. Does it not evidently appear he had these designs in view, in his transactions with Adam, with Noah, with Abraham, with Moses, in the ministry of the prophets, in the ministry of Christ and his apostles, and in the ministry of the Gospel in all ages.

Thus, my friend, I have endeavoured to answer your queries. I am very far from wishing you to take for granted that what I have said is true. Diligently search the Scriptures for yourself, and earnestly pray for the illumination of the Spirit to guide you into all truth. For my own part, I have derived much satisfaction on the subject, by perusing the works of those three eminent divines, whose theological sentiments were much alike, and who wrote much in defense, and against the abuse of the doctrines of grace; the late Reverend Dr. Williams, Andrew Fuller, and Thomas Scott.

In searching after truth, use, my young friend, all the human helps you can procure, but call no man master on earth, and endeavour to detach your mind as much as possible from all human systems. "Unto the word, and unto the testimony." In thinking and speaking of the sufferings of Immanuel, what holy awe, and godly fear should fill our hearts, lest we should be guilty of speaking or thinking unbecomingly. The subject doubtless contains unfathomable depths. O that it may prove our daily concern experimentally to know him, and the power of his resurrection, and the fellowship of his sufferings being made conformable unto his death.

Yours, &c,

JOHN ROBERTS

Llanbrynmair